YOUNG, QUEER, AND DEAD

A BIOGRAPHY OF SAN FRANCISCO'S MOST OVERLOOKED SERIAL KILLER, THE DOODLER

REAGAN MARTIN

Absolute Crime Press
ANAHEIM, CALIFORNIA

Copyright © 2019 by Minute Help, Inc.

All rights reserved. No part of this publication may be reproduced, distributed or transmitted in any form or by any means, including photocopying, recording, or other electronic or mechanical methods, without the prior written permission of the publisher, except in the case of brief quotations embodied in critical reviews and certain other noncommercial uses permitted by copyright law.

Contents

About Absolute Crime 1

Prologue 2

The Beginning 7

The Break 15

The Let Down 20

More Murders 27

The Body Count Rises 39

The Discovery 46

New Interest 54

The Aftermath 61

Bibliography 68

About Absolute Crime

Absolute Crime publishes only the best true crime literature. Our focus is on the crimes that you've probably never heard of, but you are fascinated to read more about. With each engaging and gripping story, we try to let readers relive moments in history that some people have tried to forget.

Remember, our books are not meant for the faint at heart. We don't hold back--if a crime is bloody, we let the words splatter across the page so you can experience the crime in the most horrifying way!

If you enjoy this book, please visit our homepage (www.AbsoluteCrime.com) to see other books we offer; if you have any feedback, we'd love to hear from you!

Prologue

San Francisco, California, the city by the bay. It conjures up images of The Golden Gate Bridge, Alcatraz Island, Pier 39 and Fisherman's Wharf. It's a city rich in history and culture, with top rated museums, cable cars, trendy shops and boutiques and the famed Chinatown District.

The city was nearly devastated in 1908 by the great San Francisco earthquake, which toppled buildings and ruptured gas lines, igniting hundreds of fires that burned out of control. With water mains destroyed, the fires burned for days, leaving the city in ruins. But San Franciscans quickly rebuilt, and the city has become one of the top tourist destinations in the world.

But San Francisco, like all major cities, also has history that tourists aren't readily aware of. Dark and evil predators have called The Bay Area home, and used it to commit some of the most heinous crimes in history.

In 1895 Theo Durrant, a young, good-looking medical student, brutally raped and murdered two young girls, hiding their butchered bodies in The Emmanuel Baptist Church. Quickly tried and convicted of both murders, Theo Durrant was hung at San Quentin Prison on January 7, 1898.

In September of 1921, film star Roscoe 'Fatty' Arbuckle was falsely accused of savagely raping and subsequently causing the death of aspiring actress Virginia Rappe in a downtown San Francisco hotel. Arbuckle was never convicted of this crime, but the scandal was enough to ruin his career for good.

The Durrant and Arbuckle cases were considered 'crimes of the century', and kept San Franciscans glued to their newspapers and eager for more. But by the time the mid-twentieth century rolled around, the city was dealing with a different breed of killer, the likes of which it had never seen before. So bizarre and unusual was this new type of criminal that law enforcement officers would coin a new phrase specifically to identify them; serial killers.

San Francisco's introduction to serial killers began in the 1960's with The Zodiac Killer, a phantom psychopath who murdered brutally, and indiscriminately, and left the city in a near state of panic. The Zodiac shot, stabbed, and maimed his victims, all the while taunting the police with bizarre letters and highly intricate cryptograms. And he has never been caught.

By the time the 1970's arrived, and while The Zodiac was still causing mayhem, San Francisco found itself dealing with another series of crimes attributed to this new breed of serial killer.

The Zebra Killings, a series of grotesque acts of violence, terrified the city and caused wide scale panic. Perpetrated against men, women and children, the crimes were committed by a group of radicals who stabbed, shot and hacked their victims to death.

But The Zodiac and Zebra were not the only killers roaming San Francisco at the time. Another dark and evil entity stalked the city's streets, committing crimes every bit as vicious and gruesome as any that came before him. This killer targeted the gay community, and his name was The Doodler.

[1]
The Beginning

It all began in January 1974, when San Francisco police, responding to an urgent call, discovered the murdered body of what, at first glance, appeared to be a young female. Upon closer examination, however, it soon became apparent that this victim was not a woman, but a man made up to look like one.

The crime scene was horrific, the room splattered and drenched in blood, the body slashed and horribly mutilated. Investigators soon discovered that the victim was a known transvestite who frequented the area's gay bars and clubs. He was also a regular at the city's popular gay bath houses, where men could go to pick up strangers for sex. While investigating the death, police learned that the victim had last been seen at a gay bar in the company of a young white male with light brown hair. But further investigation failed to produce any witnesses who knew who the young man was. Police continued to visit the different gay establishments and question people further, but information and clues were scarce, and the case soon went cold.

Within months, however, the badly mutilated bodies of four more transvestites would be discovered, sliced, stabbed, and butchered in a grotesque manner. Obviously connected, the police theorized that they were dealing with a sick and twisted psycho who had a deep hatred for cross-dressing drag queens. All of the victims were homosexual and well-known customers of the Bay Area gay establishments. None of them had been hesitant to pick up lovers on the spur of the moment, a fact that hampered the investigation from the start. When police would question one of the men's known lovers, they would invariably be given the names of several more the victim was known to be intimate with. As for the strangers he may have picked up, no one had a clue as to who they might be, nor how many of them there were.

Police were worried, and frustrated, realizing early on that a good portion of the city of San Francisco could be considered suspects. Worse yet, they had no idea if the killer was gay or straight, or even targeting the homosexual community. There was always the chance that he was a straight guy who had picked up a transvestite believing it was a woman, and then, humiliated and enraged when he found out the truth, decided to do away with any cross dressing drag queen he came across. For now, police had no choice but to keep following up on any leads and questioning whoever they could. They didn't know what else to do.

As winter gave way to spring, and then to summer, San Francisco police continued to hunt for the killer targeting area transvestites, but no new victims had surfaced, nor any new suspects, and cops were running out of leads. As a result, the investigation was cursory at best. Besides, the police had newer problems to worry about as an entirely different set of bodies began turning up. These new murder victims were all men too, and, what's more, they were all gay. Furthermore, they were also regular patrons of the gay bars, clubs and bath houses in the community, and unafraid to pick up strangers when the whim struck them. But these new victims were not transvestites, although police quickly learned that they too had a secret kinky side.

These new murdered men, although not into cross-dressing, were deeply involved with S&M, or sadomasochism. Not a readily known subject in 1974, S&M is a bizarre form of sexual relations where pleasure is either given, or received, from inflicting pain. S&M often includes whips, chains and bondage.

Although there were several similarities between these new deaths and the transvestite killings, there were differences as well. While both sets of victims were gay and known to pick up strangers in the same bars and clubs, these new victims were also known to frequent the more bizarre establishments in the gay community. These clubs were known as 'leather bars', and sported names such as 'The Ramrod', 'The Fe-Be's', and 'Folsom Poison'. Each of the men had been brutally cut, slashed and stabbed in a similar fashion, but they had not been mutilated as the transvestites had been. It was this fact alone that police focused on. So convinced were officials that the original five victims were the result of someone with an uncontrollable rage against transvestites, not gays in general, that they immediately discounted the idea of any connection between those deaths and these new ones.

And so, two separate investigations were begun, and the San Francisco police department was scouring the city for two separate and distinct killers.

The barbaric murders had generated little publicity, and area newspapers barely even reported on them, a fact that both angered and upset the gay community. San Francisco, in the early 1970's, had a large homosexual population, and they felt the police and public didn't care that members of their community were being slaughtered on a regular basis. Local gays felt betrayed by the lack of publicity, and believed that the majority of citizens felt the men had gotten what they deserved. In other words, they believed the attitude of the public to be; they asked for it by choosing the lifestyles they had. Determined not to let law enforcement forget about them, gay community members criticized the police, demanding the crimes receive the same attention they would if the victim's had been 'straight'.

In all actuality, the gay community may have been right. Only one known victim of the 'The Doodler' caused even a hint of a stir in the media. When a well-known, wealthy and respected San Francisco attorney was found hacked to death in his posh and expensive high-rise apartment, his death was reported in area newspapers. But when the attorney's gruesome murder became linked with the other S&M cases, the publicity just as quickly dropped from sight.

By the time fall and winter arrived, the S&M body count now stood at six, one more than the dead transvestites, and police were no closer to catching either of the two perceived killers. To make matters worse, more bodies were turning up. But unlike the transvestites and the sadomasochists, these new dead men were all upscale San Francisco businessmen. Wealthy, respected, and well-liked, most of them were described as the last person you would ever expect to be murdered. Police were also relieved to find that none of them were known to have a 'secret, side'.

Investigators worked these cases more closely, and quickly learned that although it didn't appear that these victims had any secret, or kinky, sides, they did, indeed have them. These men too, like all the previous ones, were gay and known to frequent the gay establishments looking for sex and one night stands. This information came from people who knew them well. People who knew them better, in fact, then their own families did. Street people, hustlers, and fellow patrons of the bars and clubs the victims visited. For these men were still 'in the closet', not publicizing their sexual preferences, even to their families or closest friends.

The fact that these new murder victims were gay, however, mattered little to the San Francisco police department. These men were not cross-dressers, drag queens, or into sadomasochistic sex. Therefore it stood to reason; their deaths could in no way be related to the previous ones. Right? As in the first and second string of murders, a third investigation, focusing on a suspect that targeted gay men, was now begun.

[2]
THE BREAK

While police conducted three separate investigations and searched for three unconnected killers, the gay community of San Francisco seethed in silent anger, worrying who the maniac might be that was so blatantly killing members their own.

By September of 1975, 'The Doodler' had assaulted a total of 17, and killed 14. Police had visited countless bars and clubs and bath houses. They had questioned scores of individuals, and put hundreds of miles on their vehicles chasing down leads, all to no avail. But police were soon to get a lucky break. By the fall of 1975, police had in their presence, three different men who had escaped from a knife wielding attacker and lived to tell about it.

The three men were well educated, highly respected, and absolutely terrified of more than just their close brush with death. Frightened and chain smoking, each of the men told an eerily similar story of their encounter with a young artist they had met in a gay bar. The man had been white, young, probably in his early twenties, with longish brown hair and a boyishly cute face. He had been pleasant, charming, and totally unassuming. Each man had allowed himself to be picked up by the stranger, envisioning a joyful and orgasmic night of sex.

But it hadn't worked out that way. Not quite, anyways. Once alone with their new young lover, the three survivors told the police that the man had asked permission to do a sketch of them before their lovemaking session began. All three agreed, and the brown haired youth had drawn away, creating a very good likeness of his subjects, before engaging in sex with them. Once the sex was over, however, the young man had instantly changed. Brandishing a knife, he had attacked his lovers, slashing and stabbing, wielding the weapon as if in a blind rage. To the men, he appeared to be in a rabid frenzy, grunting and growling as he swung the large butcher knife, trying to kill them. Each of the men had been injured, sustaining stab wounds and slashes from the knife's glittery blade. But luckily, each had also been able to fight off their attacker and escape, providing a description of their assailant to the police.

All three men related the story of the man sketching them before sex, though it's unclear just when this sketching had taken place. Some papers reported that the young artist would use this ruse to lure his victims into a conversation, drawing caricature portraits of them while still in the bar where they had met. Others reported that beautiful charcoal sketches of the deceased men would be found at the murder sites. Regardless of where these portraits were drawn, all three men confirmed that the young artist had, indeed, sketched them before sex, and this both excited and intrigued the investigators working their case.

SFPD was aware of the fact that sketches had been made of previous victims, and descriptions from witnesses at the bars, where some of the men were last seen leaving with a stranger, matched that of the young artist. Reluctantly, and somewhat embarrassed, police finally began to wonder if all the hacked and butchered bodies of the fourteen gay men might actually be connected. It was a hard pill for officials to swallow, having wasted vast amounts of time, energy and resources tracking down three individual killers when all along it was only one they had been after. But the discovery of the three surviving witnesses, and the information about the sketches, finally convinced them. Berating themselves for their failure, it was now that they decided to give their unknown serial killer a name. No one actually remembers who came up with the title, but from now on their killer would be called The Doodler.

San Francisco police were excited and energized and flying high. With three survivors and a description of their attacker, they believed it was only a matter of time before the killer they were hunting was caught and convicted. The Bay Area's gay community felt the same way, and they collectively breathed a sigh of relief. Once police connected all the murders, things just seemed to fall into place.

[3]
THE LET DOWN

In early 1976, police finally focused on a suspect in The Doodler murders. The man was a young, artistic sort, with a history of mental illness relating to sexual problems. It is unclear how police first focused on this man, but what is clear is that his doctor became involved with authorities investigating the Doodler crimes, and that event nearly broke the case wide open. Whether the suspect's psychiatrist contacted the police, or the man first became a suspect and police contacted his doctor, matters little. The fact remains that officers interrogated the artist's psychiatrist and learned some startling facts.

The doctor told police that his patient had been treated extensively for difficulties dealing with his sexuality. All indications are that the Doodler was a homosexual, but deeply embarrassed and ashamed of this fact. He felt no attraction to women, and wanted to be with men, but he hated himself for having this yearning and considered himself weak and pathetic whenever he gave in to it. If he was a religious man, he probably took solace in the verse; the spirit is willing but the flesh is weak.

The Doodler's sexual experience would be a vicious cycle to him, where the pleasures he desired gave no real pleasure at all, only feelings of hopelessness and despair. The doctor believed his patient to have a latent hatred for all gay men, and a burning wish to destroy them. The Doodler would most likely blame his partner for his own lack of control when it came to sexual encounters.

Police were excited. The artist's physical description fit their suspect, and his mental condition meshed perfectly with what they had already assumed, but there was more that the doctor had to tell them. His patient had actually confessed the slayings to him, and had readily agreed that he was the killer now known as The Doodler! He had admitted that he had savagely stabbed to death the fourteen gay men, after picking them up in different establishments, and also confessed that he had attempted to kill the three survivors who had managed to escape.

After listening to all of this, police promptly brought their suspect in and arranged to have him appear in a lineup. Then, rounding up two of the three survivors, (the third one had already left town), police had them view the lineup. Immediately the two survivors picked the young artist as the man who had attacked them. Police were elated that their main suspect, the mental patient with the sexual problems, had been identified, but they were careful not show it to their witnesses. Instead, they asked the two men if they were certain that this was the man who had attacked them. Both witnesses nodded their heads. They were positive. Overjoyed by this news, police prepared to arrest their suspect and charge him with 14 counts of murder and 3 counts of attempted murder. They told the two witnesses to keep in touch with them as they would be needed to testify in court. And with that statement, the officer's bubble burst.

Both witnesses immediately refused, shaking their heads emphatically. There was absolutely no way they would ever testify in front of a jury, they told the astounded officers. Police were dumbfounded and totally unprepared for this scenario. These two men had just identified the young man who had tried to kill them, and who had, most likely, murdered at least fourteen people. Of course they had to testify, this was their chance to get this psycho killer off the street. But the two men were steadfast in their refusal. One of them was a well known entertainer, and the other a highly respected business man (The third survivor, who would also refuse to testify against the young artist, was, of all things, a diplomat). These men tried to explain to the authorities that no one knew they were gay, and they wanted to keep it that way. 'Coming out of the closet', so to speak, could cost them their jobs, their careers and their reputations; not to mention that admitting to being a homosexual could also be detrimental to their health.

It seems absolutely incredible today that these three men, who had nearly been murdered themselves, would just let a sick and twisted serial killer go free out of fear for their reputations. But back in the 1960's and '70's, homosexuality was viewed in a much harsher light than it is today. In the 1960's, being gay was considered not only criminal, but also the result of a mental disorder. Males, as well as females, with a same sex attraction, were sometimes recommended and encouraged to undergo 'treatment' to instill a 'cure'. In men, this would often mean electroshock therapy, or neutering. This view had softened somewhat by the time the 1970's arrived, but it was still a confusing time for young gay people. With AIDS not yet in the picture, gay clubs and bath houses opening up all over, and gay bars increasing in popularity, many people were 'coming out' with a vengeance. But there were still many others who wanted to keep their secret, especially the older, more established men who had hidden their sexual preferences for years.

San Francisco's Haight-Ashbury may have tolerated the free love of the '60's, but it was not yet prepared for free love of the same sex.

Although police desperately pleaded with the men to reconsider their decision not to testify, it did little good. Each of them stuck to their guns and adamantly refused.

Hoping the witnesses might eventually change their minds police hauled in their suspect and put him through a grueling interrogation. The young artist spoke freely with investigators, remaining calm and unfettered throughout the questioning. Many of his answers tended to show a deep loathing towards homosexuals, and although investigators brought him to the brink of a confession many times, the suspect always pulled back. He would not confess to being 'The Doodler', or a killer, or even a homosexual. About the only thing cops actually got him to admit to was that he had 'experimented with homosexuality'. The suspect was strange, seeming to immensely enjoy his time being questioned, and relish in the attention he was getting.

Police were stymied on how to proceed. Although they would question their suspect several more times, becoming more and more convinced that he was, indeed, their killer, without the testimony of the three surviving witnesses, they were unable to arrest him. Though they kept their suspect under surveillance, their hands were tied. And once again, The Doodler case went cold.

[4]
MORE MURDERS

Police may have been sure that their suspect was responsible for those fourteen murders committed in San Francisco, but was he responsible for any others? Law enforcement knew that for many years, in the state of California, a number of homosexuals had been turning up dead. And they had no idea if any of them may, or may not, have been victims of The Doodler.

Although the majority of these other slain men were found in Southern California, and many of their MO's (modus operandi) didn't match The Doodler's, SFPD was reluctant to rule him out as a suspect. After their failed fiasco of assuming there were three separate killers earlier, they weren't taking any chances. It was always possible that their killer visited different areas, or drove long miles to pick up different victims. These other murders had a lot in common with The Doodler's, and so SFPD began the tedious job of trying to find a connection between him and the dead men left dumped around the state.

The killings had begun all the way back in September of 1971 when thirty-year-old gay bartender, Wayne Dukette, disappeared. His nude body was discovered on October 5th, but was so badly decomposed that a cause of death could not be determined. Believing his death to be an isolated incident that did not involve foul play, police did not investigate it and not much was reported on it. Eventually however, he would come to be linked with the rest of the butchered bodies strewn around the state.

A little more than a year after the discovery of Dukette, on December 26, 1972, the battered body of twenty-year-old Edward D. Moore, a Marine stationed at Camp Pendleton, was found beside the 405 Freeway. Moore, on leave from the base, had last been seen on Christmas Eve, and was a known homosexual said to frequent gay bars and clubs. The condition of his battered body gave the appearance of having been thrown from a moving vehicle, and during his autopsy, it was determined that Moore's wrists and ankles had been bound, and he had been both beaten and strangled. In addition, someone had forced a foreign object up his rectum. It appeared that the body had been re-dressed before being dumped along the roadside. Police would later state that they believed Moore had been strangled during some type of sadomasochist sex act, although they were unwilling to elaborate on why they felt this.

One month later, on February 2, 1973, the nude body of a young male was found strangled and beaten, also along the side of a busy Freeway. Although police could not identify the youth, some of those questioned remembered seeing him in several of the area gay bars. Two months later, on April 14, 1973, a second young male was found in Huntington Beach, tied up and mutilated. Autopsy results revealed the horrific nature of his death. The young man had been suffocated, but before he had died, he had been castrated alive, up to thirty minutes before his death. The man had shoulder length brown hair, and numerous tattoos, and appeared to be in his late teens to early twenties. Despite this detailed description, police were unable to identify the man.

Less than one week later, on April 22, 1973, three sealed trash bags were discovered along another California Freeway. Upon opening the bags, investigators found a gruesome sight; two severed arms in one, a right leg in another, and a torso in the third. Three days later, on April 25, the dismembered body's left leg was discovered in a trash bin outside a gay bar in Sunset Beach. The very next day, April 26, a worker at a waste facility got the shock of his life. While sorting paper waste on a conveyer belt, the worker picked up a bin, dumped it on the belt, and was shocked to see a head go rolling down the conveyer. The head was one of the most grisly sights lawmen had ever seen. Showing horrific signs of torture and abuse, the man had had his eyelids removed, possibly while still alive so he would be forced to watch the rest of him be dismemberment. Doctors determined the man had died from strangulation, and although police would fail to identify him, several of those questioned also remembered this man hanging out in the area's gay bars and clubs. Police were appalled at the savagery of the murder, and baffled by all the young men turning up dead and mutilated.

San Francisco police looked closely at these murders, wondering if any of them could be the work of The Doodler. Many at SFPD argued that they weren't. The Doodler liked to use a knife, they noted, while these men had been strangled and suffocated. But others weren't so sure. Clearly, a knife had been used in these crimes, if only to inflict torture, not to kill, and each of the dead men had ties to the gay lifestyle. Those at SFPD who supported the theory that The Doodler could be involved were also quick to point out that the majority of these killings, if not all of them, had elements of sadomasochism, or other bizarre sex acts. But others on the force weren't buying it. So what, they argued, these crimes had happened too far away, and the victims weren't slashed and hacked to death like the fourteen they had in the Bay Area.

It was true that these killings had happened hundreds of miles from San Francisco, but those officers who still thought there might be a connection to The Doodler paid little attention to that. Who knew how far a killer might go to obtain his preferred victim? (In fact, it would eventually be proven that serial killers were known to troll for victims, traveling hundreds and hundreds of miles, even venturing into other states, to find them.) And who was to say a murderer would never change his method of killing? He could be deliberately changing it just to throw police off his trail. Look at the two major cases their department was investigating right now, they argued. The Zodiac killer had shot some of his victims, but stabbed others, and those damn Zebra killers had hacked some to death with a machete, stabbed others, and shot still more. Just because these crimes had different features than their victims, that didn't mean The Doodler couldn't have been involved.

With that thought in mind, SFPD investigators continued to look at the slew of other homosexual men who had been brutally murdered in the state of California.

Three months after the severed corpse had been found in the trash bags, the strangled and beaten body of twenty-one year old Ronald Weibe was discovered on July 30, 1973, along a Freeway near Seal Beach. Weibe had vanished after leaving a bar, and had been sexually mutilated.

Six months later, on Christmas Eve, a woman taking a leisurely stroll along San Francisco's Ocean Beach made a gruesome discovery. The nude body of a young man wrapped in plastic, tied with a rope and placed in a piece of canvas, floated in the early morning surf. The body was missing its hands, feet and head. There was also a gaping wound in his stomach, perhaps made, police theorized, in the hopes that it would release the decomposing gas and the body would sink. The young man has never been identified.

Only four days later, on December 29, a new victim surfaced. At that time, twenty-three-year-old Vincento Cruz Meastas, a gay City University student studying medical technology, was found in the San Bernardino foothills horribly mutilated. Meastas had been tortured and strangled, his hands severed from his arms, and his body covered in cuts and burns. His intestines had also been ruptured and were protruding from his stomach. Meastas had last been seen on December 26th, and was identified by a tattoo of the astrological sign Virgo on his foot.

Five months later, on May 20, 1974, an unidentified man in his early twenties was discovered near the city of Carson. The body showed signs of horrific torture, and had been beheaded.

The very next month, Malcolm Little, a twenty-year-old truck driver from Selma Alabama, who was visiting his brother in Long Beach, disappeared after he was dropped off near a Freeway. Little had planned to hitchhike back to Alabama, but instead, his nude and battered body was discovered on June 2, 1974, sexually posed and mutilated, just off a lonely desert road.

Only twenty days later, Roger Dickerson, a nineteen year old Marine, vanished after leaving a bar on June 21, 1974. Dickerson told fellow drinkers he was heading for Los Angeles, but he never even made it to his car. Instead, his strangled and sexually assaulted body was found the next day.

Once again, certain officers in the San Francisco Police Department were convinced that The Doodler could be responsible for at least some of the murders. Mutilation had been an element in almost every one of these unsolved crimes, and The Doodler had shown his skill in this area with the original five transvestites he had killed. And after listening to what the lead investigator on the cases in Long Beach had to say, SFPD became even more convinced.

Detective Sargent J.J. Hurlbirt issued a statement claiming that homosexual killings were on the increase, especially in California, where the laws had been relaxed. By making homosexual laws more permissive, he stressed, these types of deaths would become even more common. This comment would infuriate the gay community, who felt that it was just another way to instill prejudice against them and keep lawmakers, as well as the public, from aiding their plight. Hurlbirt went on to add that the Long Beach connections, and the ties to that city's gay community, didn't necessarily mean that the killer lived in the city, or that he was homosexual. It was true, the Sargent continued, that the killer certainly preyed on homosexuals and engaged in homosexual activity with his victims, but that didn't mean he, himself, was gay.

For those in the SFPD, it was the last part of Hurlbirt's speech that they found most interesting. Hurlbirt ended his statement by saying that the homosexuals who frequented the Long Beach area were from all over. It wasn't unusual to find homosexuals who live in San Francisco spending considerable time in Long Beach gay bars and clubs. The local establishments advertised in San Francisco magazines, and they, (San Franciscans), held their gay balls in Long Beach. Hurlbirt concluded by saying that more and more homosexuals were gathering in Southern California, and particularly Long Beach, and that they were easy targets for thugs. Because of this, law enforcement believed there was bound to be more violence.

San Francisco officers were convinced that The Doodler was gay, and if he was, he surely would have known about the homosexual explosion in Long Beach. What would stop him from going down there to check out the action? Absolutely nothing, they concluded. In fact, they were certain that he would have gone down to southern California to investigate.

Working diligently, those in the SFPD who believed there could be a link to the Doodler desperately tried to find a connection between him and any of these unsolved murder victims. They checked their suspect's credit cards and phone records, trying to discover if he had made any recent, or previous, trips to southern California that might coincide with any of the murders. They questioned his family and friends about it too, but so far they had had no luck. They had no intention of giving up however. Just because he hadn't used his credit card, or told anyone he was going, didn't mean he hadn't been there. For now, they would keep looking.

[5]
THE BODY COUNT RISES

While law enforcement throughout the state scrambled to come up with a solution to their unsolved gay murders and put a killer behind bars, the body count continued to soar.

Twenty-six year old Thomas Paxton Lee was a San Pedro waiter who enjoyed visiting gay bars and clubs. His nude and strangled body was found sprawled half way down an embankment, along two Long Beach roads, on August 3, 1974. He had been gruesomely mutilated. Only two weeks later, another body, that of Gary Condova, twenty-three years old, was also found nude and strangled in Long Beach.

October passed without a body showing up, and November started off quietly, too. Police breathed a sigh of relief at the break, but quickly realized it was only temporary. On Thanksgiving Day, November 28, 1974, nineteen-year-old James Reeves attended a gay community church where he helped serve dinner to the needy. After helping clean up after the meal, James told his fellow volunteers that he was headed out to see a movie, drove away in his automobile, and disappeared. His car was found abandoned in a parking lot the next day, and his body was discovered shortly after that.

On January 2, 1975, seventeen year old John Leras left his house to visit a nearby roller skating rink and vanished. His body was found the next day floating in the surf at Sunset Beach. He had been tied up and beaten, and during his autopsy, doctors found not water, but sand, in his lungs, indicating that he had died a horrible death by having his face pushed into the beach sand until he suffocated.

January 17 brought the discovery of Craig Victor Jonaites, a twenty-four year old Long Beach resident whose strangled and beaten body was found dumped in a construction site near the Pacific Coast Highway.

In February, an archeologist discovered the nude, dismembered body of a young boy, shot in the head and stuffed in a sealed trash bag near the U.S. / Mexico border. The body was later identified as thirteen year old John Demchik, who had last been seen hitchhiking back in June of 1973.

On April 13, 1975 the nude body of twenty-one year old Albert Rivera, who made his home in Los Angeles, was found shot and mutilated sixteen miles east of San Juan Capistrano. His body had been stuffed into a large plastic garbage bag and sealed neatly with filament tape.

Police were working overtime, trying to put an end to all these unsolved murders, and to fend off attacks by the public and press. People were demanding the police arrest someone for these heinous crimes. Area newspapers ran ads almost daily, offering rewards for a solution to the murders, and still the body count continued to rise.

May 8, 1975 dawned a beautiful, sunny day. Perfect weather, three teenagers decided, to head out to the beach and look for starfish. What they found instead was a battered and severed head, jammed in a shore jetty, one thousand feet into the water. It would take six days, and the use of dental records, to identify this victim as nineteen year old Keith Crotwell, who had last been seen at Belmont Shore.

On January 3, 1976 the body of a Pocatello Idaho man was found on the Bedford Peak in the Saddleback Mountains. Identified as twenty-two year old Mark Howard Halls, who had been visiting California at the time, he had been strangled and butchered.

Nineteen year old Timothy Ingham, from Merced, was found shot to death on September 24, 1976 near Borrego Springs, and three months later, on December 18, 1976, nineteen year old Paul Fuchs disappeared from Long Beach. Although Fuchs body has never been found, police believe him to be connected to the other gay murders discovered in the area.

On January 24, 1977 police found the nude body of twenty-eight year old Nicholas Hernandez on a San Diego overpass near the Los Angeles International Airport. He had been shot in the head and his body concealed in a large black trash bag.

On February 28, 1977 the nude and mutilated body of twenty-four year old Arturo Marquez, from Oxnard, was found near a road in the mountainous region of Banning. Marquez had disappeared six months earlier.

Investigators were both appalled and exceedingly frustrated by all the gay men turning up dead and murdered around the state. Along with the known victims, there had been other bodies discovered that had not been identified. These included a young boy, thirteen to sixteen years old, found on August 22, 1976, very near to where the body of Albert Rivera had been found, a young man of about twenty, found on October 6, 1977 only a mile from the teenager, and a seventeen to twenty year old found on U.S. Highway 80.

All of the killings had similarities, but they also had differences, too. When San Francisco police included The Doodler crimes in the list, they still felt he couldn't be ruled out, for several reasons. Most of the victims had ties to the gay community, as had The Doodler's. Many of the bodies were badly mutilated; others were not, just like The Doodler's. Some were stabbed to death, as were all of The Doodler's victims. But it was impossible for SFPD not to see the glaring differences, too.

The Southern California men had died in several different ways; by stabbing, strangulation, suffocation, and gunshot wounds. Some were found in trash bags, some were not. Some were dumped in openly public places, while others were left in deserted areas. It got so that police weren't sure if they were dealing with one, two, or ten different killers. It was the worst mass killing spree in the history of the state, and law enforcement officers had no idea how to proceed. They had done everything they could think of to do. The had questioned scores of people, given countless polygraph tests to countless suspects, hauled in every known ex-con, and those with past mental problems, and subjected them to grueling interrogations. They put hundreds of miles on their vehicles tracking down leads, and nursed blisters on their feet from hitting the pavement for hours at a time. And all of it had produced nothing. By the time New Year's Day of 1977 rolled around, police were no closer to catching the elusive killer than they had been six years earlier when the bodies first began showing up.

[6]
THE DISCOVERY

The New Year would bring changes for the frustrated investigators, and the terrified general public, although at the time they did not know this.

On March 13, 1977, seventeen-year-old John Otis LaMay told a friend he was going to Redondo Beach to see a man named Dave, who he had met in Los Angeles. When John failed to return home that night, his mother reported him missing to the police.

Officers were initially lax in their investigation of the missing teen, assuming that the boy had probably gone off with friends some place and would show up soon. But on March 18, 1977, they changed their tune. Responding to reports of 'trash' being dumped along the side of a road near Temescal Canyon, police arrived to note a foul odor permeating the scene. There was an 80 gallon oil drum sitting on the highway shoulder, with two large, black plastic trash bags resting on the ground beside it, each carefully sealed with packing tape. Kneeling down, almost overwhelmed by the stench, one of the officers noted that the bags were leaking a putrid and nauseating substance.

Collecting their cargo evidence, police hauled the bags and the oil drum down to the crime lab where, upon opening them, they were greeted with a most gruesome sight. Each bag contained the severed remains of a young white male. When the oil drum was finally opened, police found, crammed inside, three more identical black trash bags, all neatly sealed, and containing what appeared to be the rest of the dismembered youth. The scene was macabre, each body part having been completely drained of blood and washed clean.

Was it John Otis LaMay? Investigators thought it probably was, but the body's head was missing so it was impossible to be sure.

Still, under the assumption that it was the missing teen, police began investigating his disappearance in earnest. And, for the very first time, they had some physical evidence to work with. Adhering to the tape used to seal the plastic trash bags, forensic experts found hair and fibers clinging to the residue.

Detectives had learned that John LaMay was openly gay, and because he had told a friend he was going to see someone named Dave, who lived in Redondo Beach and whom he had met in Los Angeles, officers began checking the sign in sheets at all the gay clubs and bath houses in LA and surrounding areas. Before long they came across a name that had been signed in over and over again. The man had provided a Redondo Beach address, and his name was David Hill.

Arriving at the address Hill had listed on the sign in sheets, investigators found two men living there, both in their mid-thirties. The couple introduced themselves as thirty-four year old David Hill and thirty-eight year old Patrick Kearney. They were admitted homosexuals who had lived together as a couple since 1967.

When police revealed their purpose in visiting, each man appeared relaxed and at ease, yet overly concerned about the missing youth. Both, however, denied having seen the boy.

While speaking to Hill and Kearney, a sharp eyed detective noted that their carpeting appeared to match the fibers found on the tape, and also noticed that the two men owned a dog which was allowed inside. Surreptitiously, the Officer leaned over and plucked a few samples from the living room rug. Shortly, the detectives thanked the two men and left, grateful that they weren't leaving empty handed.

Rushing the carpet fibers to the crime lab, police held their breath while criminalists compared them to the samples found stuck on the tape residue from the trash bags. They were a perfect match. Returning to Kearney and Hill's house, officers asked the two men if they might be willing to let them take hair samples from their dog, and, if it wasn't too inconvenient, pubic hair from their bodies. The two men cooperated fully and readily agreed.

Once again the police waited at the crime lab, the suspense nearly killing them, until forensic experts gave them their results. All three samples, the carpet fibers, the dog hair, and the pubic hair were a perfect match to the evidence found on the tape residue. Overjoyed, cops delayed their high fives and slaps on the back, just long enough to obtain a search warrant. Then they rushed back to Kearney and Hill's home, only to find that the two men had fled.

Searching the premises, police found a hacksaw containing a brand new blade. But upon closer inspection, they could see that the tool still had blood and tissue, visible to the naked eye, encrusted in the nooks and crannies near the handle. The bathroom appeared clean and tidy at first glance, but when investigators used forensic testing on it, it revealed a massive amount of blood that had recently been shed there.

Proceeding to Kearney's place of employment (he had an excellent job as an aeronautical engineer with Hughes Aircraft), detectives found the exact same type, and brand, of trash bags used in the disposal of the young boys remains, and the same type of filament tape used to seal the trash bags.

The very next day, Hughes Aircraft would receive a hastily written letter of resignation from now former employee Patrick Kearney. David Hill had been unemployed, preferring to stay at home and be the 'housewife' in the relationship.

Police were both excited and relieved by the discovery of Kearney and Hill. John LaMays murder so closely matched several others, that the connection was almost inescapable. Other bodies had shown up in the same type of trash bags, and having seen the two suspects, it seemed obvious that they would have had to work in conjunction together. Kearney was a little punk, appearing small, thin and frail. Officers doubted he could have handled the young, strong men that had turned up dead. He would have needed help. Finally, investigators allowed themselves a little hope that they might have finally stumbled on a solution to all the murdered men who had been scattered around the state.

On April 22, 1977 the Riverside Coroner's office finally identified the headless body as that of seventeen-year-old John Otis LaMay. Long before the use of DNA, chemists still used blood analysis, along with a scar from a birthmark on his left knee, to make the identification. Police now had the evidence they needed to bring in their suspects, and they immediately issued warrants for the arrest of David Hill and Patrick Kearney.

But where were they?

Hill and Kearney had disappeared, as thoroughly as the missing and murdered men in the state of California had, and they were nowhere to be found. Their pictures graced the covers of many newspapers, and stared silently from wanted posters all across the state. Their family members were hauled into police headquarters and interrogated numerous times, all the while insisting they had no idea where the pair was hiding out.

While police searched for the duo, they quietly continued to build a case against the two men. Officers believed they had more than enough to convict them on the LaMay murder, but they were also gathering evidence on others as well. Eventually they would find enough to charge the two suspects with two counts of murder.

On July 7, 1977 Patrick Kearney and David Hill walked into the Riverside County Sheriff's office, pointed to a wanted poster bearing their pictures, and told the stunned officer that they were them. The duo had fled to El Paso after cops had taken the hair and fiber samples from their homes, but being on the run was not for them. They were tired of hiding, and felt sorry for the way their families were being treated. Both men felt it best to just give up and get it over with.

Finally, for lawmen, an answer as to who had been killing all these men in California might now be within reach.

[7]
NEW INTEREST

SFPD found they were feeling mixed emotions when Riverside County took Kearney and Hill into custody. They found themselves disappointed because neither of the men was the young artist they suspected of being The Doodler, yet happy that two vicious killers were off the streets. Intermingled with those feelings came a ray of hope. Maybe they had been wrong about the artist being The Doodler. Maybe Kearney and Hill had been making trips to San Francisco to find victims, too.

Since the fall of 1975, when The Doodler's last known victim was discovered, until now, SFPD had quietly worked the case, looking into these other murders, and keeping tabs on their artist suspect. But others in the city barely gave the killer a second thought. Those in the gay community remembered, of course, but The Doodler story had never been big news, and the majority of the general public had forgotten all about the unknown killer who stalked the city less than two years ago. But in July of 1977, when Patrick Kearney and David Hill were arrested on suspicion of killing 28 young gay men, interest in The Doodler resurfaced.

From the moment that Kearney and Hill were taken into custody, interest in The Doodler was immediate and intense. The San Francisco Police Department was inundated with phone calls and visitors, all asking the same question. Was Patrick Kearney or David Hill The Doodler? The press was relentless; their presence uncomfortably felt each time an officer walked out the door.

By this time, police knew that the duo in custody was not The Doodler. They had quickly shown the three surviving witnesses of The Doodler attacks pictures of Kearney and Hill, and each had failed to identify either of them as the man who had attacked them.

This had been a tough blow to the SFPD, who had hoped the arrest of Kearney and Hill would finally close the books on their fourteen unsolved murders. But it was not to be, and in an effort to get reporters, as well as the public, off their backs, San Francisco investigator Rotea Gilford spoke publicly about the case, revealing for the first time information that had never been made public before.

Gilford told his listeners that for the past year police had been questioning a young artist about the 14 slayings and three assaults that had taken place in the Bay Area between January 1974 and September 1975. The young man had been cooperative and had spoken freely with the police, he said, but had never confessed to the killings. Although a confession had not been obtained, Gilford continued, SFPD was fairly certain that they had the right man.

Asked to explain that comment, Gilford related the story of the three survivors, all victims of a vicious knife attack, who had picked the artist out of a line up and identified him as their attempted murderer.

Stunned by this revelation, the press demanded to know why the killer had not yet been arrested. Reluctantly, Gilford explained that the three surviving witnesses refused to testify, adding that they were hesitant to come out of the closet and publicize their sexual proclivities. Without their testimony, he stressed, prosecutors could never convict the youth, nor could police even charge him with the crimes.

Reporters, as well as the general public itself, were aghast at these revelations, and they demanded to know how these three victims could just let a deranged and vicious serial killer get away scot-free.

Gilford explained that it was their right not to testify, even if ordered to do so, and then went on to explain about the three survivors being well-connected and important people. But the press and public didn't care about that, and they were less than satisfied. Disgusted, they shouted at the detective to arrest the suspect anyway.

Gilford shook his head, telling them that it would do no good. They did not have the evidence to arrest the man. He did admit though, that if even one of the three survivors would be willing to testify, SFPD could charge him. That seemed unlikely though, he added, since the entertainer had left town, and at present his whereabouts were unknown, and the diplomat was extremely angry about the investigation and refused to cooperate. The businessman too, had left town and was refusing to answer any phone calls or letters from the police.

Although it seemed hopeless to those listening, Gilford knew that there was still a chance. SFPD was aware that if there was a weak link in the survivors, it was the businessman, and police were not about to do anything to jeopardize their relationship with him. The detective adamantly refused to furnish the press with any clues to this survivor's identity.

Gilford also refused to reveal who the suspect was, but he did give those anxious for answers an ominous conclusion to his speech. The suspect, Gilford said, was still living in the Bay Area, although not in San Francisco, and surprisingly, he had a steady lady friend. Gilford went on to add, somewhat chillingly, that similar murders had ceased since the suspect told police he had been 'cured' of his homosexuality.

Harvey Milk, a San Francisco gay rights activist, tried to defend the surviving witness' decision not to testify, stating that he could understand their position, and that he respected the pressure society had put on them. He added that many homosexuals kept their sexual preference a secret, because they feared losing their jobs. They had to stay in their 'closet', Milk continued, noting that there were some 85,000 homosexuals in San Francisco, and estimating that 20 – 25% of them hid their sexual proclivities. This was especially true, he continued, of the rich and powerful; doctors, lawyers, politicians and the like.

Another gay rights activist also spoke up, but he apparently felt that identifying The Doodler as being homosexual was detrimental to the gay community. Hank Wilson, a teacher, went on to say that the case represented societies 'double standards' in dealing with crimes involving homosexuals. Angrily, he claimed that the press never publicized the heterosexual murderer who killed twelve women after raping them, and added that the gay community had diversity, too. There were crazies among them, he said, that was true, but they dwelled within every other part of society also.

Immediately after the police released all of this information, the story of the Doodler and his crimes disappeared once again from the newspapers, and apparently from the minds of the general public as well. Members of the gay community were angered and disappointed by that. They would never forget. Yet they remained immensely hopeful at the same time. They truly believed that at least one of the survivors would eventually do the right thing and agree to testify. All they had do was bide their time and wait.

None of them ever dreamed that nearly four decades later they'd still be waiting.

The Aftermath

None of the three surviving witnesses of The Doodler crimes has ever come forward to identify him. The fact that none of these men, all victims of a savage knife attack that nearly killed them, would be unwilling to testify against their assailant is, perhaps, one of the most intriguing aspects of this case today.

The diplomat may be a lost cause, but it is doubtful that the entertainer is still a popular and public figure, and the respected businessman has certainly long since retired. If these men are still alive, and either of them decided to come forward now, surely no one would vilify them for their sexual preferences. Homosexuality is no longer a taboo, as it was in the early 1970's, and reputations are no longer ruined by admitting to being one. Do these three men realize that The Doodler could still be arrested and tried for his crimes? There is no statute of limitations on the charge of murder. Perhaps one day, when they are facing their own death and want to cleanse their conscience, one of these men will 'man' up and do the right thing.

The Doodler himself has never been caught, and it is unknown whether he is alive or dead. Nor is it known whether he has ever killed again. If he is alive, The Doodler would be somewhere in his early to mid-sixties today, and quite possibly still be engaging in one night stands with other gay men. If so, it seems likely that he would not be the one picking up strangers anymore. Chances are, young street hustlers, very much like himself in his youth, would be doing the soliciting, and almost certainly not because of any attraction, but in the hopes of getting money or something else from him. It would be interesting to know if The Doodler is still sketching his lovers as he did while committing the murders.

It is unclear just how long police kept tabs on the young artist they were convinced was The Doodler, or if they might still be keeping tabs on him now. Detective Rotea Gilbert died in 1998, and The Doodler has not been reported on in almost forty years.

Patrick Kearney and David Hill were charged and arraigned with two counts of murder in the first degree, and a judge ordered them held on $500,000 bond each. When Riverside County District Attorney Byron Morton took his case before a grand jury, he got his indictment on Kearney, but surprisingly, the grand jury refused to indict David Hill and he was released from custody.

Hill immediately left the state for Texas, and Kearney pled not guilty to the two charges. Later however, Kearney changed his plea to guilty, against the advice of his attorney, and gave a full confession to his crimes. He stated that he had worked alone, and that Hill had known nothing about the killings.

Kearney claimed that his passion was necrophilia, or having sex with dead bodies, and that he killed his victims to satisfy this urge. Questioned about torture, or picking up marines, Kearney knew exactly what the police were getting at, and he vehemently denied it. He was not the Freeway Killer, he stressed, nor had he ever participated in torture. Kearney was aware of the other killer, the strangler, who was working the area at the same time, and he appeared miffed that the police might think it was him.

Kearney told law enforcement officers that he targeted victims that reminded him of the kids who used to bully him as a youth. He preferred his men to be blonde, arrogant, and good-looking. He either picked these men up in gay bars, or found them hitchhiking along the freeways. Once he had them in his truck, he would quickly shoot them in the head to incapacitate them. Kearney was a small man, and would not have been able to subdue his much stronger victims.

Once he had killed them, he continued, he would strip their dead bodies and have sex with them. Sometimes, Kearney admitted, he would be overcome with an uncontrollable rage, and would beat the dead bodies to assuage his anger. Once calm again, he would dismember his victims in the bathtub, using towels to soak up the leaking blood.

On the day that John Otis LaMay came over to visit, David Hill was not at home. Kearney invited him in anyways, and, just because he felt like it, shot the boy in the head as he sat on their living room couch. He then dismembered the youth in the bathroom, packaged his body parts in the black trash bags, and tried to stuff him into the 80-gallon oil drum. But only three of the bags would fit, and he was forced to leave the others on the side of the road with the drum. He admitted to being absolutely terrified when police showed up at his door inquiring about the missing teen.

Kearney would eventually confess to 21 murders, and receive 21 life sentences, the death penalty not being an option at the time he committed his crimes. He is still serving his sentence today in a California prison.

All the dead men in Southern California found shot and stuffed into trash bags were the work of Patrick Kearney, and he became known as the Trash Bag Killer. The other bodies, those so horribly tortured, were attributed to Randall Steven Kraft, the Freeway Killer. Kraft, however, would not be captured until 1987, and he would continue to kill right up until that time. Kraft was later sentenced to death, and is still awaiting execution on death row.

The Doodler case has long since fallen into obscurity, and it is unclear why he never received the publicity that other serial killers of his caliber had. The Zodiac killer, who terrorized the Bay Area at the same time, was reported in the press almost daily, and The Zebra Killings, while not as visible as the Zodiac is today, were also well covered when they happened. But The Doodler barely even rated a mention. Could it be that the gay community was right when they claimed police didn't view homosexual victims as 'worthy' as others? The

Zodiac killed nice, respectable white people, and so did The Zebra Killers, but The Doodler killed gays, transvestites and men with a penchant for bizarre sex practices. Did that make a difference in the press coverage? Perhaps it did, because nothing much was ever written about The Doodler, and even today, with computers and the internet, it is almost impossible to find out any information about this killer.

Looking at these crimes today, and knowing what we now do about serial killers, it's easy to see how confusing those crimes must have been to both the SFPD and other law enforcement agencies. These were rare and unusual crimes, and investigators were unsure of how to work them. Yet police learned quickly, and the advancements that have been made in tracking and catching these predators today have been remarkable.

But the 1970's were a different era, and a different time, and serial killers were a 'new' breed of murderer. Unfortunately, they are all too common now.

Bibliography

Oakland California Tribune December 25, 1973

Long Beach California Independent Press Telegram January 4, 1974

Long Beach California Independent Press Telegram June 8, 1974

Pasadena California Star News June 11, 1975

Corona California Daily Independent April 22, 1977

Van Nuys California Valley News June 22, 1977

The San Mateo Times California July 8, 1977

The San Mateo Times California July 9, 1977

Corona California Daily Independent July 11, 1977

Oxnard California Press Courier July 4, 1977

Santa Ana California Orange County Register May 11, 1987

www.ingramcontent.com/pod-product-compliance
Lightning Source LLC
Chambersburg PA
CBHW020303030426
42336CB00010B/882